A Cast of Tens

David Bromige

Avec Books

Penngrove

Also by David Bromige:

The Gathering
Please, Like Me
The Ends of the Earth
The Quivering Roadway
Threads
The Wise Men Drawn to Wonder by the Fact
  So of Itself [with Robert Kelly and Diane Wakoski]
Three Stories
Ten Years in the Making
Birds of the West
Tight Corners & What's Around Them
Out of My Hands
Spells & Blessings
Credences of Winter
Living in Advance [with Paul de Barros,
  Barry Gifford, Sherril Jaffe, Ray Neinstein, Gordon
  Pilkington, et al.]
Six of One, Half a Dozen of the Other
My Poetry
P-E-A-C-E
In the Uneven Steps of Hung-Chow
It's the Same Only Different/The Melancholy
 Owed Categories
Red Hats
You See (Parts I and II) [with Opal Nations]
Desire: Selected Poems 1963-1987
A Sampler [with Stanley Crawford and Irene Wanner]
Men, Women & Vehicles: Prose Works
Tiny Courts
They Ate
The Harbormaster of Hong Kong
Romantic Traceries

A Cast of Tens

Grateful acknowledgment is made to the editors
of the following publications in which some of
these poems first appeared: *Avec, Fragmente, Hole,
River City, Sulfur* and *That.*

ISBN: 1-880713-01-2

Library of Congress Catalog Card Number: 93-71879
FIRST EDITION

Cover art by Michael Costantini.

Note: The misspellings in this text are intentional.

Avec Books
P.O. Box 1059
Penngrove, CA 94951

for the words Poetry and Ent-stellung

Quién hace tánta bulla...

Author's Note

Rather than wisdom texts, expressivistic witness, or formal nonsense (though these modes in pieces obtain here), these poems are constructed to be specula. The impasto which the other modes create through explaining, hectoring, celebrating, denouncing, or concealing, in these compositions occurs where different subsets of language collide. These moments, which are widespread, are distributed fairly evenly throughout, anti-climactic. It is to this evenness, itself thanks to the author's points-of-view having been ground from self-aggrandizement, to grit to glass, that the poems owe their speculative and specular nature. If you are as a reader indifferent, they will prove an indifferent read; if you are ugly, and find ugliness repulsive, these will repel you.

To intervene to this end, an arbitrary (=symbolic) means of clustering has been employed—3-3-3-1 for instance, or 5-[x]-2, or *1*-2-3-*1*-3, or 2-3-2-2-1, and so on.

'On a Hundred-Block Walk' constantly shifts the pattern; 'Dictation' constantly reduces the count stanza by stanza. (A stanza throughout this book comprises ten lines, however clustered in their sub-stanzas; or better to say that the sub-stanzas make a ten appear at the next level of organization, whether actually as in most cases, or imaginatively as in 5-[x]-2 'Night' or the diminishing 'Dictation.') In the composing, the awareness of each pattern generates via expectation and anticipation various phrasings (exactly as will iambic pentameter or trochaic tetrameter; my method has fewer echoic invasions). The habituated self's expression is curbed by a newer habit.

Otherwise, and as with all my books, these poems would be exemplary in their concern for those who struggle (or not) to come to life in our time, who feel the adventure of the universe and the race (and its clusterings, its societies) depends on the ability to listen, and who wonder, during such summary, what is being represented and what is being ob-scured.

David Bromige
Sebastopol, September 25, 1993

Contents

OCC. HAZ.

All torque and no accent
The phone rings, and he converges
bent above his runes

chiseling away what isn't his
in a parallel way. A person believes
to abstain from sex

will make you ill.
You are ill. 'Mai hone
naytyer stayzay

misteri to mi.' Nipples instance

specificity. What she wants
was him, what he wants
perpetually escaping him

And here 'we' project and displace
That mountain they climbed more
than once. 'The crmnl maind'

thinks rigidly without the law
T measures rational practice;
D, density. Stick that in, bring death

The forbidden conformity

perpetually escaping. Ever
Ready Emblem Company
had these matches printed up

on hill in Tenn., the forbidding
commodity either famous or luminous
Either the pure or the beautiful

One head viewed from back
shocked itself as mirrored door
swung of own motion

'Didn't hear mi calling!?'

Being more X than K
'Feet don't fail mi, miaow'
Carved above the grave

'Curved above the groove'
Some horrible laborers come
for the duration. The cat's jaws

The diminishing amount of kibble
To remove whatever we are not
availing ourselves of. Some small detail

from some minutes of mad flight

Some passage devoted to motion
A raft, by night—the dash
and the function of the dash

And the calling of attention
And would you save or live your life
Ineligibility become a question of background

along with legibility
The beauty is in the failure
whose pieces come by mail

to Ed at the local factory

NIGHT (WITH *I* FOR THE STAR)

Resolves into horizontal bands
The sedate walk of the Categorical Imperative
Our servants cover the remainder
One pulls on a rope
that activates the bell

that tugs at our ears
that draw(s) out our lives

The inexplicable and the unexplained
Some things are too important
Starry night of the classics
The verb formed from constellation
So that 'Once upon a rime'

Mercy had anticipated sin
One dwelling much as another

They wear the same outfits
Resentment treads heavily
and our ceiling is its floor
Of the supernumerous welling
faking its accidents

Their beauty that of flowers not fruit
Consumed by our Founder

Odd turns we take, so many glottal stops
So many grotty loops
How hamletlike a lens
'…That all the old stories…'
Draw a circle and draw a circle

They were wasted in the square
The composition of the little panes

What price fame? The grave awaits
The ways of lighting same the same
Having no idea where it may lead
(God going beyond in His ways…)
'I feel my father looking down on me'

These chairs were made in our image?
In the image of those we obey

So many years of victory
resulting in defeat
The page turns indecipherable
'All we can take is what we've given away'
We can't speak of the display

Except what it reminds one of
Of the masking love

Washed over by these waves of the indifferent
Beauty, beauty, beauty, beauty
A single swatch of green identically
'That looks on intensity and never sees'
Salt instancing contagion, indicates

This life among the new illiterate
matters—to whom insist—the self

ANOTHER REFUSAL TO MOURN

Moon through bamboo's cling curtain

Yellow post-its hide some text
to which attention is thus drawn

The impression of one's life (one life)
as clarity produces certain cruces
besides, of course, Chapter One

'I can explain everything'

Followed by the word *But*
'Finding a mess for the mess'
But then the wife and the child come home

Provide an example, it will be

but as to the what. . .
Your forensic novel, Watson

was erotic. Drove himself
to the hospital, demonstrating
the good sense in a state of shock

Moon still in curtain but higher

'We must feel all threads are in our hands'
'Not that I don't enjoy seeing you
having fun with an object'

Stuck pins in the eyes in a snapshot of himself he gave her

We say something about surrogate
for the revealer's delight

Is yellow hopeful by analogy
with sun or spectrum
Saying something about surrogate

Weaving of analogy a nest

Like spelling 'levitation'
in a ward that gravity
has slowly filled with the deaf

Check—this is initialled

You are initial too, or better
Anterior that registration

'The invention'—check
'Not the invention'—check
'The intervention'—pause

Lettering thought replacing pain

as a hand turns a page
He hears twin as they say 'kin'
Nothing when they utter 'other '

Textuality: a doorwedge

That is one in a series that point
at a car becomes paranoid language

The astonishment of what you thought
is manifesting that cry that parting
breaks into two bands

Overlapping yet discrete

in the story that is boring
into his breast. He thinks about hair
—everyone does—it covers things up

One begins noticing convergence

He decides what's pertinent
and evinces fair-mindedness

within those outlines she denies
That must have meant space
giving that term a good shake

In the story the ants help / The stories always get off

(Look who they get off)
The neighborhood is amused or amusing
Abusing one for misreading

Experts declared the photo of a ghost

Only for fear of saying more
or even less the opposite

You are about to identify
with a shrug of resignation
'You have unlimited time'

Weave of curtain loses appeal

The answering machine strikes dumb
You need something to count on
that doesn't feel like a sore thumb

POETIC INTERMISSION: WHEN X FLIES OUT THE WINDOW, WON'T THE PLOT RESOLVE?

Won't the music swell
The moon fair on the channel
This empty cup mean emptiness no more
'I live by feeding the desire
to escape the present'
The soul be a raven and fly free
a lightly developed negative
unpredictable even for evil
X: 'You're in such a curious position'
—supine, décolleté

Why do you always follow me
follow along the horizon line
That is our guarantee
The private eye
may remark the 2 ells in alliterate
on a scale that's infallible
an Arabic ding
. . . these irregular signals . . .
For the dead to wound the unknown
they must risk life

'and Paradise may be figurable'
24 sounds like 26
I am x, x is a cs
Fishes wash flesh
I shall and I should
We fail an algebra of presences
Stirred against my better judgement
by this putrid chord succession
Eyebeams cross, fire flickers
X gets us to erase his prints

Stirred against the backdrop clifftop
nothing keeps coming between
with only skull and sky above
XPICTOC, XPICTOC
which is actually a memory—morbid
It was the wind—perhaps
2 women, 1 man—a shadow
2 women, 1 mirror—3 women
Then one misses several portions
Indian rope trick's ridiculous predictability

and the surface breaking, reforming, brilliant
'We must have Reality, no matter the hardships.
 I mean by Reality, that which we invoke the EVERY-
DAY to save us from. For the everyday is
habitual and habit an insulation. All those dishes!
The degree of initiation we experience—'
Then several parts go right through one
Dreams have been true (Come, now)
In between, the rings
All x is is Alexis? No—more

What we can't see, her eyes caress
A door swings slowly open upon darkness
This coroner may be unbribable
This private eye infallible
Society or these scattered phrases
stand for the accidental
(she rolls down the cliff, up the map)
in love—'celestial companionship
through all eternity'—with X
'My dear, we are infinitely near'

Sea is my other, not prime
The cart before the cart
on which the understanding relies
'You've got to be logical about this'
X smashes the fusebox
to break the Liebestod
' . . . and would go free'
And the grand piano, simply
(lights cigaret to distance self from X)
X—allows time to get ready, count

('Excited? Nervous?') to discern the real motive
(' . . . must have Reality, no matter—')
The police would sooner run him in
2 persons, 1 mirror (opaque)—3 people
Id orders its representations
eggs the letter on its sound
in obsolete December
just when any sign is powerless—the real thing!
Tinsel star, incense smoke, theatrical illumination
'Garrulous with me? Nix!'

But Mr. X smokes pipe, sports tie
centering the storm
Moon is one, and ocean
Then one misses several frames
for you are the projective versa
Behind the sign, the man
(The past we had thought dead, plots against us)
2 men—1 bow tie
Get to bed, forget about it
If we are 2 together, for a spell, then (sister) let's

Yet wasn't that merely a rime?
We don't know what troubles the servants
'I'll leave you alone with your—objectivity'
Call for the Freud Squad—squalid
Hard—honesty—to show us ourselves
But it can't be supernatural as long as x is ours
and not-ours, but what about our
Substitute for the missing piece
Aspirated voiceless Ionian velar
Raising the dead in a mirror

WHILE KNITTING

Water was trickling somewhere
But then it was simply the clock

Here comes your spouse
who, once upon a time
was quite unknown to you

In this photograph of your birthplace
no cars can be seen on the street

Only horses and some carts they draw
Yet your entrance began in a taxi

Now you know the word necessary

What was browner about the past
is a quality of ink and paper

A function of time
and its (it is its) passage
The flesh sags at the elbow

Did the Welsh accent colonize India?
Schubert played Beethoven

In the movie last night
allowed itself to be replaced

You will not find this refundable

Quality depends on conjunction
'Destiny feels so special'

Why we imagine sequence
and the legal meaning
of a moment

'Until I fall in love
all my existence is rectangular'

He was inarticulate
in an attractive sense

his names come from Latin

So much of her thigh showed
Fifteen years must have gone by

The church has a facade
meant to set off faces
as transitory phenomena

Then you discover you share birthdays
Like thunder and lightning

And can leave a lot unspoken
What did they see from the train

And what did they notice

Lonely bubbles leave the head
in alienating long-distance shots

Vast city with its vistas
has no need of us
yet without us is vacant and still

Dancing as an idea is odd
Much as clothing in a tropical zone

Or that he likes or dislikes her ears
or the crosses on the graves

The history of the word 'like'

The telephone in Greek
could signify labyrinth in Spanish

While *I* am a caryatid
for the palace in the square
we uphold doesn't care

Here comes the mail
but no letter from your spouse

How well does she know you
for that matter, Luis

Nuestra, Nuestro—many kinds of snow

Do pesos drop, and how many?
Dawns break into any language

bringing its thoughts of itselves
The one saying much, the one saying nada
The one saying madrugada

How what the words convey
means less than the picture-squares

of touch—in the mind
where all can be counted on

Alone, where surprise stays unlikely

NEVER ALONE

Hush that presages expectancy
A kick in the teeth
The rushed motion to the far horizon

Everybody loves those stars
So resembling areolae

Then there's Deserve
Next to Do it to him

All these v's and k's
even the mute hears
alone in the scarlet field

that is yellow to him
But the unused days won't flush
nor the stories wash

concerning a biography
never the point

More to the purpose
is the animal mask

Nor never quite not
Faint down covers the cheeks
The eye is a whale's

From polled willows, swords protrude
Step off the transport into anywhere
'Happiest in country settings'

Where he can float up in quotes
Detached from the text

as the phenomenon would have it
The farcical characters

the elders take as law
But the string declares it a kite
—in his pocket, a church

English 'U' accent felt best
for cultural instruction
describing the class act it all is

Red orange rooves and groves
silver and twisted

'Greensleeves' silvers the mourners
as if these were downs

Poplars sheer pigment and lindens
planted in lines—a popular arrangement
says the historico-botanical agent

Empty? Restful
Vacant? Exciting
'But that mauve with the gold

reconciles'—if beached boats
watch those sails, then

which group are we?
Sun on our backs

The triceps and biceps
Veils, the axillary tufts
The courtyard filling with a single mimosa

We are dead long since, says someone
as the wreckers' ball topples a wall
that had mattered a lot

The pictures loom in
over conversant furniture

Sheep are everywhere
Pastoral, sails rime with souls

Nature permits him purple and gold
pigments, chunks of the stuff
sliver the boards of the floor

(We used 'silver' before)
For who has seen the wind
and shown same, the mummy

gesticulating from the attic
Gesticulating from the attic

while Socrates brings the mail
by the beard of Socialism

Nor does beer affect the glass
Where the bottle's blue, the bar is too
Maison d'amour with a straight face?

The house has a conscience
Only the table casts a shadow
And each object is isolate

in this previous Paradise
to choice, sleeping hoodlums in sad space

reduce to color. Shape. Line
as in 'Appenine' on 'Lurline'

Monumental work—bad taste
smothered in flowers that fade
and flowers that stay paint

Trees twist up out of earth,
clouds corkscrew, lineaments
must be decided if they melt,

transmute—evidence (=F)
dictates to experience (=X)

as they come to arrest
the tantamount sleeper whose dreams

lost them money. Color
to say something
What is the color of something

or the sign of design?
Faces are bits in a crowd
yet eyes guide as candles

The beard feels redder this morning
to the terror in the mirror

The boughs will break,
the slates scatter

the people below—always below—
the malady—'imprinted in this place'—
'don't tell me she isn't Symbolist!'—the clock

has no hands for a reason
She waits there, past the last
crow, but is about to knock

and speak to his parents
Bits of brightness make up lots

Out of a clear blue sky
And there, in view of several people

although further down the beach
—took it out—smooth, warm,
large as life—to play with

THE TWO OF ROCKS

The old man is 112 pages long
and so is the sea
They are deeply symbolic (psychotic)

But we who are a rock and a rake
to the insinuations of sound and
in among the trees
where the rocks look back

Those trucks haul a city
to punctuate not thought
Yet the drawing of the sorts

Of persons we are, as we say, instances
The completely depressing were an achievement
presence defeats

And joy—as for that
'My mother was lost inside herself'
One wanted to be locked up
Surroundings disappear, the face

assumes the mirror
of highly polished stone
But you always moved

A foot kicks a pamphlet
brought who knows how
to this rare spot

'Orgasm completes a circuit
Or you deteriorate
Love the one you're with'
(It's ripped and smudged)

'Peel back that hide
Let one another's beauty in'
And you always moved

'Bury the third' then poison or person
'Lumbar ganglia' 'Solar plexus'
'Carpe' and then probably 'diem'

but possibly 'dream'
They laugh when they read this
Their eyes fill, tears
course down their cheeks

Who can bear a crying child?
And who is not a child
Yet the 'you' always moved

A moment collected, swelled, dropped
and in evaporating, noticed lips
as well as a handful of bored holes

Accents are metaphysical
The Swedish film is dubbed with Swedish accents
The typewriter sounds like breaking sticks
Two read a letter—one reads, one listens

A reader attends, in mind
The car seen from above (if cameras see)
'A shot so I can die' (if love can...)

She manages a smile
about then, about then
The syncopated ticking of two clocks

'Raised by words meaning nothing really'
B Minus, B Major
'Get me some metaphors—I'll glisten'
Then the notion you never love anyone

except in those ways of theirs
meaning nothing really
His narrator's face fills the frame

In its own wake or shank
'The little faith I have'
The screen darkens to go blank

Commanding attention
along the one horizon
with terror of the unseen
And of his command of the words

telling him this is it
The family version
that these rocks contradict

The cock nosing up the channel
sounds like history beside the dance
the cells of history proclaim

The evidentiary skin
in certainty whereof
we touch, relinquish, touch
People being what they are

'I can't recall my mother in motion—
only bits and pieces, frozen'
He asks for her fingers

In his, a hope
A pebble to worry
To be wrapped up in

They touch nipples, material
The bark of trees
Even confession screens
'…Dead, were it not alive'

From these high hills, the myth
flows through gully, over stone
as though ocean-drawn

Where the cards are being
laid out. This and this
contradict—impossible

But mind those two places
at once—no reassurance
were of sufficient plausibility
These trees arrested these rocks

With thematic nausea
The laurel turns viridian
The rays themselves have walked

As the writer has to believe
In her text, scenes form:
Satyr and nymph root and grunt

'I sat through this before'
The next card 'like a rock cast in the sea'
He is remembering his name
and how it sounded once

In a witches' dictionary
Items of archeological significance
We hope the Indians will win

Trucks crush the uprising
We can leave, we are sane

COMMENTARY TO 'THE TWO OF ROCKS'

We use the same materials
Inside and out for unity
and can't leave this circle

'It becomes desirable to pause'...
Said the man who lived in a quarry
to the woman who lived and lived
and lived in a tree ('No one I think')

When death is survived
Do you become calm
as a thing unnameable

The rules are altering
as you play along by then
what? murmured the ancient tome

About then one listener slept
while another slipped and stripped
The possession of a name (to me)
and the possibility of being named

(Being, named...) They sought privacy
in a church, as in a nonsense verse
letters vainly think to hide

The speaker is supererogatory
What then of her words
These necessaries?

'I can take it or leave it alone'
Head riddled with metaphysical darts
The body inside washed with blood
like the site of a murder

Surroundings disappear, the face
luminous for the shadows
He'll watch while she says anything

is everything. 'When I was in pain
I tried to remember pleasure'
Flowers, bulbs and breathing

You recall the child
you in some sense have been?
Only in glimpses
You recall your love?

So like a landscape
this absence
as if only one

sits whittling, whistling
(We do this for unity)
Weighing six to eight syllables

as the pain-pills wear off
While the word starts up
and up in the open meadow
bounds and rebounds to those sounds

and singing of bones
Hidden in loam by epochs
was to practice restraint

W-s t Prc-c rStrt
upon the view from the myth
The chains of cause and effect

harrow the meadow, an odor
whereby one floated (crushed leaves of bay)
Passion feeds the heavy stars
Abstinence the years of their light

Crushed

Passion

        from the myth

cause and effect
the field below

whereby one floated
leaves of bay

   feeds the heavy stars
Abstinence the years of light

whose banks extrude
One that has to be for you
One for whom you regard

CULLENDER HONEY

'No one—a facility'
'My life is real—I'

These runes—what apparition
Handles towards one's hands
hurdles—the gag-order

Being generally circulated
As a friend's pain transpires
'I scribble away at midnight'
Is the question who cares

As their menhirs locate the moon

To bring 'her' back
To dwarf their mistake

'Now does everyone know what they're here for'
Reflected in still pool
and the life of its own

(They left toasters on the beach)
The best part of a life
whose only other witness dies
'. . .to kill'—add 'or. . .'

Replacing the self with the bottom line

Thought in our rhetoric
Like flies in amber laid

Listening to promptings
to step off that vehicle
from the hilarious throng

Afflicted with wisdoms
Rain of acid, etcetera
Handed to all by all
while out for a drive

While out for a ride

That wall—has to be
Someone—something likes me

Solitary discourse (man
hunches above some level
surface) nails better than a tract

The word she (Mrs.T) would render meaningless
—or Li: 'No such thing as culture'
Gobbledegook—smokescreen
—Squidink—and say, here's your check

Ear on belly's lulled by truth

Or you're cured
of uninterruptible babble

where 'of' is also 'by'
We sat by the creek
and pictured a log fire

'Whan will my eyes the light finden?'
It's bald as your knee (overly)
The length of a thigh (jocular?)
Someone will disturb you

The question must be when

People want too much
and are too good at getting same

Exploding from touch to touch
however wrecks the careful plan
The rough circle defining sane

Beauty perishes—or children
who dwelt within in your insides
never even phone—landscapes
savaged by guardian robots

He builds as the light wanes

SLOW LAKE (SKYLARK)

Quavering measure
We endure (in) another
Beat her own head on a stone
Letters come to light too late

'Toilet complete—you like?'
Owl's sounds rebound
to be counted on

'Vun day vhen ve vere junk'
But the gray-primrose hatched
dress is still apparent

'...One day'—ringing
down the curtain
Substitutes figure for feeling
The hurt has been great

So now take this
or that, he orders, passion
eats what we had for lunch

An omniscient narrator surely knows
a fountain from a portico
The desk clerk's note he fingered

Introduces local detail—
'When might *you* have used these words
in some semblance of present sequence—
or what (precious child) do you depict

imbued with them?' No piccolos play
beside the dying sea
'Leise flehen...'

The meticulous instance
Light striking down from
the sole window in that kitchen

As though nothing had happened
stokes the hell of exclusion
As a name on a roadsign
stroked the fellow on by

A variance from the map
More taken with the thought
than the words—*bonne chance!*

'Hurt you because you're dear'
As though nothing had happened
Pages of the score disperse

transforming place
Look up what it's under
What's under it
We go to measure

That which lies about us
(We are us as dreamed)
The ruler is a wand

A wandering
noun—minstrel
scholar—mind

Glance—betraying
purpose, with purpose
One repeats to shift
emphasis—lift those

pillows, those heads
that are pillows, those
marks those sounds that are

'Understanding'
Sudden slam of a door
As of a door

On the police blotter
version forces itself
to forge the law
Perjures that ignorance

which is all it can know
'This is History speaking
the words of your mouth'

'Cleft for me...'
As the tissue is turned back
The sureness of the hands

with their instruments (blithely)
Sleep sleeps
If the earth quake
wakes or denies

'It's around here somewhere'
They sit in the kitchen
They sit in the light

Bugs on a stone in a flood
Saying they did their best
the heroes stopped short so that we...

COME TO WHERE IT SITS

It's a cloud
It's a plane
It's seafog, stranger
though apparently cloud
It's a clod

That was a sound
demonstration of

Paradise as a noun
How many friends, enemies
came in close enough

to decipher the cryptic
Red lettering on burlap
stapled to the restaurant
A mouth sucks noisily
as Marianne and Ross breakfast

on melon and sausage
the man at the next table

barely copes with 500 mikes
But they use the word
'Fascist' to unbungle (their) time

He is more true because you
refuse complicity
in Hungarian and Arabic
with Lincoln and LBJ
since the age of two?

The piece proposes the puzzle
until it gets lost in a flash

She perched on the couch
while he stood on the floor
for two minutes of fucking

neither could quite remember
nor forget. Yet the clock
kept the time. A dry beach
A band of cirrus
You are liking their look

In the book being read
at the moment you read

'partial local coherence'
Modernists distort what?
A dark and stormy night—

then a square yard of earth
(with its leaves) moves
(with its twigs)...
'Was it the wine too good to be left
till last, wasn't drunk till he was?'

Brown eyes weighted with gold
framed by dark red locks

A pool of light forms
from the first of the jewels
But the dead fern and dirty moss

won't act background. The idol's lips
don't want to change
the subject. So move
'In this ruby light
you ask this open mask'

...unable to believe this
is all. 'Heaven-aspiring trees'

made him reach for his aspirin
and mediocre be the middle
of a short life. Diamonds

sparkling like drops
in the sexual hair of the returning
bathers. The dew
their moving volume shakes
'We have come to kill you'

Venus hates Psyche
It's a relation

in the heads of the returning
barbers. He liked to hear her talk
about now. 'Aimlessly'

taking dictation from the city
streets until stopped short by
what quickly proved more of the same
that this once (however) spoke her name
…bonfire smoke that 'follows' one

for there is the wind
and here is a place

to be smoked. 'I will do nothing
I do not believe in'—
'marbling' of Milky Way or foliage

WITH CHIN IN HAND

New England wants a topic
the way clematis wants a wall

He brought his pumping engine

These noises, ranging between
jouissance and chatter

She clears the ground
More than forty whacks

Old England wants a cane
plantation—I want you

all to enjoy yourselves

With everybody's money
things get pretty abstract

She attacks the words

Paper scraps—obsessional
narratives about the dog

with your tire in its teeth
—it was Mr. O'Rourke

in bedroom farce beckoned
and now you being born have to die

The words Do you gather

Outside the movie house
like signs protest too much

The feel of silk or rayon

Caress as in crotch
All fine words

Light up when something's said
best when deferring to them

His head had been getting bigger
to fit more people in

to the church of his choice

making his brain sweat
extensive advertising

to monitor attention

Serious people
since death is inescapable

We must get money
but not cynical

about our goals, reputation
for our dedication

to affording amusement

Then when the rain begins
it's just as we predicted

There are clean (t)(b)ow(e)ls for the guests

An absence of flamboyance
And a cloud to be or not

Consistently—the rub
to draw the blood

to the affected parts
has been long anticipated

and thus sweet in coming

Which leaves to be accounted for
surprise (shy to use the word 'vagina')

She knows depends on expectations

of the upshot being otherwise
arrived at than was meant

So his head gets bigger yet
This view could only be

from California
and through binoculars

Bigger than the figures focussed there

ON A HUNDRED-BLOCK WALK

Words of the sentence like people
seen from above—sentence-like streets
to see people on

Earth protected by clouds
(City by flak)
A word by its sentence

Child's play by its blocks
and blocks that spark
Trees by their park

Anxious voices shut up (thus anxious)

One by ten, ten to one

The women who work at Crocker
anxious as Wells Fargo takes over
Where are they now

Hive of the post-human humming
Pretty to picture a choir
Ugly with limbs that bend out

and glossy or dull
shells—shelves
upon which to set this or that

Dried trickles where mud was
Speak into the camera
Tell it to be kind (try to)

Now the irreparable
gives you the chance to be
human in a time-tested sense

'Even the most visual of crucifixions'

All show
all know it
is all show

To suppose is not to know
As we suppose we know
and demonstrate the magnet

'Loving you for 40 years'

For the children we were
unroll another map
than the up-to-date projection

Two times side by side sit
through an overlong movie
Heroes of the library-ship

If the bombs miss us
the city is large enough
to absorb the enemy's interest

Closing the door on perspective
Mr. Shock offers distraction
Yet when I see children today

Crawl in between me
at the expense of proper form

Not a word as to why

The single odor of a desert

flowers: 'Those nights I was happy'
To give his word for the fact
Protected by the tale

For the troublesome present

'...Harvest moon' (and then
they lay awake counting
between lightning and clockwork)

How long want the ruins
to stick around—until
we forget what they mean?

As if one might be three
if not more, and might think
for each—yet stay one

The idea it should be bad
'And you do this before the King of England?'
'But Cary Grant didn't mind' (currently outdated)

The idea it should be good

The grass = forgetfulness
The flames = exit from childhood
when all the great questions arrived

The screen = in flames
'I don't want to discuss it'

For the troublesome present

The moon (no) bigger than the clitoris

'Go away! Stop stopping me
seeing what could be here instead'

What frames the story:
non-story, sprayed on
while the band played on

The blonde strawberry, the moon blue

In a familiar section of town
feel able to alternate routes
—but where one is the city?

Down to his hairy parts: footprints
plus the right to feel his feet
via pain, minus abstraction

The pure hate of abstraction

on the body's account. 'Woman
says it, the priests steal it:
Bald, oder nie' Accept that

Except that
once in a lifetime

Turn page
Not there

Words where blood was
The scream in flames
What you actually do

would be the only story
What you had in mind

That you could look at

PROSE INTERMISSION: STILL TO START

Still a handful. How say mere./

You think he should care more, and though he knows that, he doesn't./

Three things went through his mind. Nothing changed./

Tomorrow will have those feelings its events, including memory in its/ caprice, bring in its train, to the junction. No anticipation seems/ worth the alterations thus inflicted./

Seven. Say seven. Say inflected./

Keep using it to remember what you are using it for./

For instance had been a favorite phrase, affording location to what's/ vague. Location qua traction. The rough for the smooth./

The slashes indicate where the lines broke in the original, which was composed for an 8-1/2 x 11 page.

Cartires, caterpillars, butterflies. On the stone. Yet the ivory hand/ was subtler. Not suppler. Will this longing never cease to make the/ while feel worth it?/

Febrile, inconstancy, fluxlike, noticed by some constant. Try infected./

At what rate can failure be secured, delayed. Understood./

The stone had had a Latin name. Then names not even known yet. Snapshot/ snaps shut, springs trap./

Weight ate weight, out late./

Verstanden? Nein. Nicht wahr? Ja oder nein. Ja-oder-nein./ Suffering the correction of the rest, endless in all senses./

Cartels, bagatelles, bound to a surname in cultural obligation, site of/ no escape./

To be...all argument useless. Informed hands do insane deeds. Your flesh/ and blood squawks in a fit of her imagination./

'Four men loved the pilgrim soul in you' 'Four men, that's all'/ true, yet unoetic. Maybe at once?/

Noviced by some constant. The mistake bleeps./ A spilling era. How be so mistaken, and for whom or what?/

Still, the bleep connects to a consequence, for which he must adjust./ Now run and answer it. It can't be the him they want he knows./

Sand washes into the small depresssion in the beach, sinks, and is not / anyone we know, the radio suddenly remarkably loud. Inability at certain/ speeds to discriminate two strikes on the key from three. A snake if you/ say so. A flat. It'll be sharp, searched for./

Cemetery, what makes you so difficult to spell? That beep marks error with/ an obstacle./

The webbed again. A gain? A gin./

Wherever she looked, mice in underwear. She let it rip./

Number Nine. A haunting perfume. He buried his head in his hair./

Fell, fane, labyrinthine amethyst pathways, limned with./

Desperation City, or Deportation City, followed by a zone of code,/ some precedent. They and all over./

And may all your feelings be small enough to name, to exchange for small/ sums of money, sons of mummy. What world whirled away, along the grooves/ of what history? You correct yourself by the majority, who look to you/ for the spotlessness of their laboratories, of their lambitude./

Squeak, head's heart, heaving metaphor into a mouth, some eyes or ears./

It-it was great, yet not enough. Stuttering in the teeth of Time./

Revenge senseless in a world of ones./

Ones and ones only, how erase?/

As though to persuade concerning an identity the other will then disclose/ as different in some essential respect, seduced into this revelation by/ therefore a kind of lullabye./

Plus the overwork now chronic among all lucky enough to be so plagued./

But compared to hitting the thumb with a hammer, much qualifies for the/ rubric 'abstract.' Like rueful./

When evening arrives, and the workday world melts back into the homelife, / while old songs play on the piano, how does the piano feel?/

'I do want to be liked.' The problem is there right at the start./ The cog knows nothing worth speaking of concerning the moving belt./

FORTY WHACKS

It's a language we can recognize
One of the first time

One place known in terms of another
We want to know how it was done

Possibly not, but to wonder
at the training required of us
to identify a beard

To nearly miss the obvious

They simulate the city square
mouthing the words they recall

Man in the water
unable to speak

so I speak for him
and she senses the system is working

Hot air fills the integument
We like pressure of shape
The paper is 'full' of mistake

but God wants the air in the tires to be free

Anything lends itself to endeavor
to lose the head by careful plan

Light through the double doorway
Someone comes from the sauna in the square

Nearly run down by rehearsed horses
in the mist we found pleasant, in the past

Next to the churchyard
The movie told us 'Angst'
Maybe he'll be back at my place

The unusual loosens the tongue

in the Era of Games
when the dress exposed some shoulders

That the body still the mind
that the spirit be freed

that the mind may sting the body to this
I did not care for the man

who was meant to be me
He screwed it up and threw it away
as we talked about spare parts as traps

I spoke, he considered

About the bull and the cloak
The bought ones that collapse

LEST WE FORGET

What does Sisyphus at home
and does he do it earlier

Spacing indicates what without known scale
except an own risk entered

Screams   Breath-holding

The adventures of a couch
These who will have died
The laughable mishaps of a footstool

and all that they recognized

thawed   Thought   Pulsed

Number interceded
its tray of ice

to mist the pictures
to the status of a science

An instance of memory

if such be one's present
opens again at the same page
opaque with text

of Dr. Mesmer's letters to the lorn

Naming them Isaac or Abraham

The official speech is English
but what is it in truth

but likewise English with a twist
A system including bias

A refusal   As if a door

As if a knob
Or a hand
And the hinges

and what they could recognize

opened again to the same page

Struggling to wake
between two sleeps

to invent absolution
How tattered the leaves

to the fingering signified

Deserted applied to streets
or to hearts in the hunched
homeostasis of feelings

When is wheeled on

A rainbow: a crock

When some become this
in order to resemble

fear lights on unlike forms
They rime with norms

Agony   Anguish   Our wish

that the future recognize
This, this, this, this
saying what   Of no time

A joint experience

We forgot when the time

Came   Went   Which was us
Wanting it to be us

Across whom a glib caul
had been stretched or elided

and our sexual rapport

with its Kirlian flickers
Please pass the salt
while admiring tough-mindedness

Censored (this line is)

Declining to be tortured

Could rain be pure sound
then its intervals

rinse off a ground
the hearts recognize

gathering God   the word God

Blood to symbolize
blood, its flesh
symbolized by flesh

The fingers were playful

Memory's drumskin

It's all about loss
if you need to sound right

at another's cost
you show us your lust

Revising each point of departure

Gluing the units
to be other units
to which we glue 'larger'

Discourse as a city

where one was not heard

DICTATION

Taint of what it led to

There is no choice

for the poet the compleynte

Memory bans with its comparatives

No wind today, the smoke from no one

goes straight up to nowhere

The poet who must make

something of the inevitably expressed

Memory bans with its absolutes

Supine before the velvet dark

Speak and forget

The social imperatives

Witness and adjust

The craft can be practiced

removed from certain attenuation

Music beside the charnel house

tainted by its reception

Ecstasy to forget

Sin of description

Entertainment

Advent of spring the recognizable

Words the recognizable

What it led to happened

Unreasoning and only reasonable

There can be many distractions

Sin of saying so

Sin of omitting to

Poets who sang love

incurred what it led to

No it isn't fair

'I am in this without fault'

Words that come from somewhere

tell it is (however) just

Mind is implicated, ruined

Point to the children

Others did as much

The Macaques' numbers on the increase

The range has food enough

Their offspring beautiful

Across the gulf

Market hope (soap)

(Joke) to choke

Syntax led to us

in Thesternesse

close enough to touch

Is this not closer

or altering substance

that nothing washes out

and nothing taints

But next to nothing

when dawn manifests

with its linked people

When truth and justice

leave the dictionary

sanitized

OF BILLIONS

Things filling up with zeroes

Shrinking space

A kind of human winter

Forgive me mother

you meant to say something

Look there at the rosemary

with its blue-purple aroma

Specifically social ends

lending spite and anger

Spider like the sand at Carmel

Why point in that direction

Mt. Olympus wreathed in

inspiring flagellation
flagging inspiration

While he filmed what happens

Doing what was told

Telling what was done

to get neat (add Met)

Clouds cover the sun

Disaffiliate from what

Doing what I want

Whoever that turned out to be

Imagination meets the language

The word Imagination

Tears too deep for words
Obtuse callous populists
who lost then found their sneakers

Cockroach on my foot   (Naked)

Beauty meets terror

in decalled classless no-space

Of friends a score or more

These years seldom seen

A cast of tens

Red-mauve of Process & Reality

Its atomizing Sun

A single, unified subject
would have to be a poet
with a different income
'Your currency is handsome'

And us as the outcome

Get up: work

'Upon the waters…'

'…a bottomless pit'

Thorn, thorn, prickly leaf

'Reading, the return to zero'
Strike pose: Blackberry!
(Later—still at the job)
Bring me my natural mien!
We treasure your gleam
Your thundercloud casing

And us as the narrative

Its web far from a tangle

in which one overbalances

Or now is the hour
Fractally speaking
Continuing lyric tradition
meets Modernist aporia in Keats
Claude refusing Royaumont
'The nightingales keep me awake'
Clatter of accents in the rue de la Harpe

I pucked a cousing plum

Entropy exerts its magnetism

In the garden from John
Bob and I later ate
so hmm and so hah
Here is the pit
Wit is a metaphysic
Then when I went to get help
fell for the rescuer
Wanting my children from her

I—where are they

All now here
in our habits
to say a few words
by way of exploration
'An archetypal itch'
if invisible object
fled into music
which it supports
Instrumental reason

Arms around shoulders in snapshots
No wall to hang them
that isn't taken up
Perhaps with proclamations
Perhaps with Futurism in the form of total war
Schrecklichkeit
Sticky wings
Unnaturally defined outlines
Straps and racks and chains

Only mistakes are interesting

now there are no mistakes

TO—

Ingrained by the screen
our images could not withstand

But the subtle subversiveness
of a language 'of knaves and fools'
Where of has the force of revelation

'Out of the mouths of Polish mothers'
The phones begin ringing

Attention blots out what?
And the moral high ground
where you can tell what hit you

to quit. This American thing
asserting the right to defend

a question mark
What the people will do
is think so to speak

Volumes—or frescoes,
to which she's grown immune

A tree grows in the States
Rhizomes for roots
'Scusi!' But here come some men

looking for a hero
or a knuckle sandwich

The sax is safer for the belly
laughs while the breast weeps
Emotional distraction

'Be selective—get the edge'
making an idol of production

but the closed
raises the non-included
First rimes with post

The arbitrary
to die at its own hands

writes in the ledger
of the skeleton and the chalkboard
'Do as we do…My, you're clumsy'

The signs suggest length
but can't stop being signs

That nothing will fit
except the word Assumption
Twist that into what's seen

They will display for one bodies
waking from a bad dream

where his identity was of concern
to the police breaking the door down
or neighbor gently knocking

to be beside herself
People overlook identity

by the third meeting
of a tennis ace
with a barrel of laughs

The bird in the fist
wants to hear the name

we neglected to assign
to its absolute truth
whose persistence upsets carts

of what have to be apples.
A range blue with options

of what have to be onions
(G. Greene) as the voice fades that says
it belongs to the mirage (marriage)

—Oasis, says a name near the foot
of the range. 'Not me, but…'

someone we identify with
perhaps fraudulent plausibility
as the intuition one has

tucked away in the drawer
with the key to the strongbox

Where spirit and meaning cohere
thanks (pal) to—to—
The happy endings litter the sidewalk

COMMENCEMENT EXERCISE

Not the vehicle we started out with
But all we've got left

Compadre—and some scape

Some scope (for the rime)
Snow covers the killinggrounds
It was murder or emigration

One made a model of a ship

Distance drifts
'Could face nothing
without you'   Friends

Sad now, that was horrible once
Now (just) sad like (just) sex

Cover these traces with speech

and the moment's invention
What we have left
to us, a light retreat

'Didn't grasp I was illegible'

A free man, like they say
'Hello Mister Day'
Our side now uppermost

Until such allocation shall be made
divides us side from side inside

Breasts [n., v.]

that rise, the wonder
Will we come this way again
Looking for his corpse

they save the drowning

'We believe her—he doesn't'
Space enables many tragedies
And a sleigh drawn by cockroaches

hurts their hands
Many nerves collaborate

and Mr. Pain arrives

Who mutters in the body
It is pleasant to undress
He craves to be erased

The Fair presents freaks and oddities

He stuck his tongue out and spoke
Now he was understood in Aerøskjøbing
That's why their laws

and the clear blue of their skies
draw blood beside quiet pools

Casual around important machinery

Sudden starts dedignify
When is a losing cause
complete? Boxcars of axes

What the frame allows to form

fire does to water in the hermetic
cylinder of philosophy's history
seeking for some norm

So proud to remember
The words and the deeds

Facing it alone

And to worry the word *deed*
Waves and clouds are provided
Enter the x of economics

Exit into slices of bleakness

of which there are three
—an infinity of blindingness
Divine since various

Photo by B.J. Fundaro

David Bromige lives in Sonoma County, California; he has published many books of poetry and prose fiction. He has received grants from the National Endowment for the Arts and the Canada Council; in 1988 his selected poems, *Desire* (Black Sparrow Press), won the Western States Arts Federation Book Award. Other recent books include *The Harbormaster of Hong Kong* (Sun & Moon Press), *Romantic Traceries* (Potes & Poets Press), and *Men, Women & Vehicles* (Black Sparrow Press).

A Cast of Tens was printed in December, 1993
of this edition
twenty-six are lettered and signed